The Woman at the Well

KATY MULVANEY

DEDICATION

To my mother and her many best friend priests, who all encouraged me to
go ahead and publish this thing.

Your grace was sufficient for me.

CONTENTS

Introduction: The Frog in the Pot   1

1   The Woman Using the Well in the Heat of the Day   6

2   The Woman of Samaria   13

3   The Woman Descended From Jacob   21

4   The Woman Without a Husband   25

5   The Woman Seeking Peace   29

6   The Voice Crying Out in the Center of Town   33

Conclusion: The Frog in the Ice   42

ACKNOWLEDGMENTS

Many thanks to Eleanor Hernandez for her beautiful cover art design and encouragement as I was putting this edition together.

To Monsignor William Manger for reading this in its early form.

And to Father James Dempsey, who insisted that I publish my collected thoughts on this story. Now that it's in print, I hope you believe it counts as "real."

INTRODUCTION

This book exists because a priest, faced with the gospel reading I love more than any other, delivered the only homily that has caused me to walk out of the church in anger.

I stood from the hard pew in that unwelcoming, nearly-empty echo chamber of a church and stormed out the back. I charged back to my apartment and wrote the blog post[1] that I have reworked (among many others) into this book. I wrote another one later that night, after I drove to the next town for evening mass and the priest there gave a beautiful homily. I am inspired by this story in positive and negative experiences and everything in between.

The gospel, of course, is the Samaritan Woman at the Well, which Fulton J. Sheen first taught me to love in his *Life of Christ*. The homily I walked out on substituted the intricate, remarkable story for a twentieth century parable that should have stayed in the 1950s with the pastor. Tellingly, the pastor followed the parable with hate speech and an open desire for the social "boundaries" of the 1950s.

You probably know the parable.

---

[1] Original work on this and other Bible stories can be found at Lentenreflection.blogspot.com. The post referred to here is titled "The One That Is", originally uploaded Sunday, August 28, 2011. I'm very glad to have turned the unvarnished anger in that piece into a more coherent and productive conversation.

The Frog in the Pot

Once upon a time, there was a frog in a pot on a stove. The water was cold, so the frog wasn't worried. Perhaps it wasn't as happy as it would be in a swamp, but it swam about with reasonable contentment.

As time passed, the temperature began, slowly but steadily, to rise. The frog noticed, but he wasn't concerned — or at least not as concerned as he was by the complete lack of flies in this cold, metal excuse for a swamp.

But, either over ten minutes at a rate of 3.8° Celsius[2] per minute or over ninety minutes at a rate of 0.2° Celsius[3] per minute, the temperature rose notch by notch, little by little, to a boiling point.

And then the frog died, without ever realizing it should escape the rising temperatures, since they came on so slowly.

In Defense of the Frog

Like I said, you've surely heard this parable.

It arose out of a dramatic misunderstanding of Dr. Freidrich Goltz's intention, which was actually to prove that the brain, rather than the nervous system as a whole, is in control of fight and flight responses.[4] He was comparing a (literally) brainless frog to a regular one. Guess which one didn't jump out of the pot in time…[5]

Of course, Goltz got further than Dr. Victor H. Hutchison did in 2002 at the University of Oklahoma. Hutchison rebuts the legend right at the beginning.[6] Frogs, as he found and any child could have told him, don't like being put into pots even if the water is a non-fatal temperature. Go figure.

And yet it is popular. It touches something that feels like a truth to

[2] If the frog was a victim of Dr. Friedrich Goltz in 1869.

[3] If the frog was a victim of Dr. Heinzmann in 1872.

[4] I use the common shortening of the panic responses here because it is better known and includes the only two that Dr. Goltz would have been able to actively measure. The full list of responses to danger, however, consists of fight, flight, friend, and freeze.

[5] Morgan, Ann Haven. "Temperature Senses in Frog's Skin." Harrison, Ross G, and William K. Brooks. The Journal of Experimental Zoology. New York, etc: Wiley-Liss, 1904. Print.

[6] Durham, Robert B. *Modern Folklore.* Lulu.com, 2015.

people, even if it is, scientifically speaking, a misunderstanding of an experiment comparing frogs who have and have not been decapitated.

Scientific accuracy isn't the point of a parable, of course. I would certainly never dismiss the Parable of The Sower because that's not actually how farmers plant seeds. The Frog in the Pot parable, like all parables, is a symbolic lesson. And it's the symbolic message that makes my blood boil.

When you push past the most obvious message that devastating changes usually don't happen all at once, what exactly is everything else in the parable a symbol of? Things get troubling, or at least confusing, right away when you start to examine the metaphor:

The frog stands for us, people of faith or just the "good" human beings.

The pot is the world around us.

The water can best be understood as the morals and values of our world, either put into official laws or just cultural norms.

The temperature is evil creeping slowly into our godforsaken world.

The scientist/sadist chef is…your political enemies? The devil? A beloved childhood author writing books that make witchcraft seem fun?[7]

But if those are what the different elements of the story stand for, then the message to leap out of the pot the moment that the temperature starts to creep up…means that we should exit the world? It's not like the frog can do anything else about the temperature, right?

At worst, that's a call for mass reactionary suicide, which explains the parable's appeal with destructive cult leaders. At best, it's a rejection of Jesus's mission for us to be in the world but not of the world and the call to be in the world doing good work and fighting the good fight in John 17:

> "I passed your word on to them, and the world hated them,
> because they belong to the world more than I
> belong to the world. I am not asking you to remove
> them from the world, but to protect them from the Evil One.
> They do not belong to the world any more than I belong
> to the world. Consecrate them in the truth; your word is truth.
> **As you sent me into the world, I have sent them into the world,**

---

[7] My first experience with this parable was a build-up to a condemnation of J.K. Rowling's *Harry Potter* series. Can you see why I've always hated this parable?

and for their sake I consecrate myself so that they too may be consecrated in truth. **I pray not only for these but also for those who through their teaching will come to believe.**
May they all be one, just as, Father, you are in me and I am in you, so that they may be in us so that the world may believe it was you who sent me."
John 17:14-21

Looking past the parable's most horrific message, as most people do...Do we really want to encourage people to react drastically to every slight rise in "temperature"? Are we called to throw a tantrum every time the world moves in a direction we don't like, even if it objectively does no harm to us? Do we *really* want to have the slippery slope argument every single day?

If you answered yes, then I entreat you to keep reading anyway. You are, in fact, precisely the person I want to begin a conversation with.

And perhaps you can help me with this. I've always assumed that people who would answer this question as yes are the ones who believe that there is a Goltz Figure controlling our world as the scientist did the pot. In one form or another, there is someone — a conspiracy, a villain with an evil plan, or even the Devil Himself — slowly and maniacally turning up the heat.

From my perspective, I think you would have to believe that in order to jump straight out of the world over trivia. You have to believe it is a plan or at least a trend that will eventually prove unstoppable.

Am I wrong? If there's another reason this parable resonates with you, please let me know why we should be leaping out of the world when we are in no objective danger.

If this is your reason, then allow me to humbly submit that there is no Goltz.

Consider for a moment: what if there is no Conspiracy, no intelligent enemy gradually but steadily bringing to world to a soul-boiling bubble? What if God didn't leave the Devil in charge down here?

I'll go even further. If the frog is fine in a variety of moral temperatures, isn't insisting on our personal preference, despite the harm it does to others in the pot, the opposite of a moral victory? Why march in the streets to

Make the Pot 17.5° Again when everyone is still fine at 22°? And would be for 30° of greater change!

All in all, it's a very twentieth century parable, warning of Hitler as if he were a subtle evil that no one saw coming.

The Samaritan Woman at the Well is nothing like the Frog in the Pot parable. It's true, for one thing. It's actually in the Bible for another.

But it's not just truer and Truer than the Frog in the Pot. It's the exact opposite lesson.

1 THE WOMAN USING THE WELL IN THE HEAT OF THE DAY

A Monologue to No One

I don't remember deciding to start going to the well at midday rather than at dawn with all the other women. I slept in one morning I've all but forgotten. The water was hot and unpleasant when I brought it home, but the trip had been so much easier. So much easier than enduring the gaggle of women who all came before dawn so that they could get their water home while it was still cool. Before the sun rose and baked even the mud to a burning crisp.

I didn't decide one day that I would rather have hot water to drink than deal with the gaggle of women. I just made up reasons to put off going when the water would be pleasant and everyone would be there. Then one day, I found myself lying in bed feigning sleep so that I could still stumble out to the well "late". I wasn't banned from using the well at dawn, but I was chased out all the same.

It was not always that way. When I was young and unmarried, I enjoyed the attention as older women clucked and speculated on who I would snag. I was pretty enough to move up the social ladder, but I was poor enough that I might end up with some good-for-nothing waste. A few honored matrons took it upon themselves as a holy mission to make sure that the latter didn't happen. I always enjoyed the giggles and glee

6

over an engagement, and mine was no different. And the pestering and speculation and guarded sympathies for me as a new wife.

The unending sympathy, both offhand and genuine, when my first husband died.

With the second wedding, everyone was still approving. There was almost more bustle, in fact. The matrons handed down their positive judgment: a young woman should have the chance to be a mother.

They were less sympathetic, somehow, when my second husband died.

My third marriage ended in divorce, and that's when it started. Half the talk was shielded from me behind cupped hands or in low whispers. Giving themselves by shooting furtive looks in my direction.

By the fourth man — who I never actually married, though I claimed otherwise until I almost believed it myself — I was an object lesson. Pointed out to other pretty, poor girls as a warning. A freak. No longer a member of the gaggle. No longer even a full person or resident of the town. Gawked at like some seller of foreign wonders barking in the marketplace.

By then people moved away when I set down my empty jugs. For awhile I took a perverse pleasure in the ability this gave me to cut the line if I placed myself just right. Then I realized how often my jugs were bumped and jostled so that the water slopped onto the sands. Most days I wondered home with too little water rather than deign to lower the jar again.

By the fifth husband, no one spoke directly to me. I knew they discussed me. I saw their looks, and I saw money change hands. Betting on how long this one would last. Their silence was cushioned, at first, by my husband's arms. After all the mess, I think he was the love of my life. I wished more than those women ever could have that I had found him first.

There was no support for me when he died. When I needed their sympathy, their understanding, the most.

I could hardly blame the man who kept me in his house now for refusing to marry me. What counter could their be for his "jokes" that marrying me was fatal? That taking me to temple might well unleash a *plague of locusts? "We're safe as we are," he would say. Because he never went to the well at dawn.*

Some days I wondered if they thought they could stone me, little by little, two or three rocks per day. To absolve them of having to do it all at once and square their consciences with the murder.

So when I started oversleeping, I leaned in to it. The water was warm, but the trial did not come.

It was Fulton J. Sheen, in Chapter Eight of his book *Life of Christ*, who first opened my eyes to this story. He was the first to help me picture what an outcast this woman was. This woman who has more of her words recorded in John's Gospel than any apostle but Peter. He begins with paragraphs helping us understand that she was a member of an outcast race, "No Jew would ever pronounce the world 'Samaritan', so hateful it was."[8]

He devotes only a sentence, in contrast, to our first, pivotal tip-off that she is an outcast even among the outcast people: "It was rather unusual for a woman in the East to come in the heat of day in order to draw water. The reason for this unusual conduct is to be discovered a little later."

The dispute between the Jews and Samaritans and the dispute between this woman and the rest of the town are, at their root, the same thing. It may not seem so. All of the lofty theological arguments may feel so much more important, or at least drastically different, than the instinct to shame a woman living outside of the Law of God's precepts.

They stem from the same flaw of faith.

I am going to approach my point a little obliquely this first time. One of the most important Bible stories in my family is the story of the lawyer who summarizes the Law into two rules, of which Jesus approves. In some versions of the gospel, Jesus does the summary and the lawyer recognizes it as correct. For obvious reasons, my lawyer mother and father preferred the version where the human follower understands what is important. In Luke's gospel, it appears immediately before, appropriately enough, the parable of The Good Samaritan.

---

[8] Sheen, Fulton J. *Life of Christ*. Doubleday, New York, 1958. Also: Clearly I don't hate everything that came out of the 1950s.

On one occasion, an expert in the law stood up to test Jesus.
"Teacher," he asked, "what must I do to inherit eternal life?"
"What is written in the Law?" he replied. "How do you read it?"
He answered, "Love the Lord your God with all your heart
and with all your soul and with all your strength
and with all your mind and love your neighbor as yourself."
"You have answered correctly," Jesus replied.
"Do this and you will live."
But he wanted to justify himself, so he asked Jesus,
"And who is my neighbor?"
Luke 10:26-29

In Mark, the lawyer comes off a little better. He replies not with an objection but with agreement, and Jesus pronounces him, "Not far from the kingdom of God" (Mark 12:34). For this reason, it made for a better choice to read at my father's funeral, but I must unfortunately say that I think Luke's version is truer to the minds of great lawyers.

The version in Luke strikes me as so very, very human. So devastatingly true to our default morality. This expert in the law, who has devoted his life to studying its intricacies and passing along the knowledge and wisdom he gained, comes to see the radical potential messiah in a crowd and engages in a public intellectual debate. That shows at least a desire to be open-minded.

And when asked how he reads the law, he accurately distills its central message. He does not go on about how it is a Code of Conduct From Above that sets apart forever God's Chosen People. He does not fall back on the Ten Commandments or start into a jargon-laced discussion.

He instead captures the true intent, rather than glorying in the rules themselves. Love God and love others. Jesus approves. This lawyer gets it.

And then, it turns out, he doesn't. His reaction is to seek for clarification. "Who is my neighbor?"

I mean, it can't mean *everyone*, can it?

Not people who were raised in a religion that has mutated slightly from our own so that they don't worship in Jerusalem anymore, right? Not the people who intermarried after Israel was conquered and they were left behind when others were taken into slavery? Not the "mongrel semi-alien race," as Sheen problematically calls them?

He's looking for exceptions, loopholes, or at least a clarification of when he's allowed to judge those neighbors. That's a lawyer's job, after all: to seek or enforce clarity and consistency in each individual case of the law.

The response he gets is the most famous of Jesus's parables, although I seldom think we realize just how radical it is anymore. After describing a priest and a Levite leaving a robbed man broken by the side of the road and a Samaritan who patched him up and paid his bills, Jesus asks the lawyer:

> "Which of these three do you think was a neighbor
> to the man who fell into the hands of the robbers?"
> The expert in the law replied, "The one who had mercy on him."
> Jesus told him, "Go and do likewise."
> Luke 10:36-37

Sheen interpreted the phrasing of the response as the lawyer not quite being able to bring himself to say that the Samaritan was the hero of the story. That seems valid, in its way. He can't quite bring himself to say that the "mongrel" was the better Jew. That the "semi-alien" was the better person of faith than the figures of the temple: the priest and the Levite.

Of course, it could mean that the lawyer finally understood that it is our acts of kindness, not our official religion or our politics or anything else that would fit on a Facebook profile that defines if we are living in accordance with God's teachings. The Samaritan is the one who understood that we are all one people and all accountable to one another.

But then, that's just another way of defining who it is that we're allowed to judge and who it is that we're supposed to help.

I can just imagine the lawyer's internal monologue: *So...you're saying that we're allowed to judge those who don't help those in need? Those who go around sinning? I mean sure, we won't spit on nice Samaritans, fine, but we can still shame women who have five husbands or tax collectors who betray our nation or people whose sins cause their babies to be born blind?*

If the lawyer did take this message from Jesus's parable, I hope he was also around for the Woman Caught in Adultery, when Jesus shut down the idea that we can stone those who commit sins with impunity (John 8:1-11).

The same sin links prejudice against Samaritans and the ostracism that would have led the Samaritan Woman to go to the well in the heat of the day, when she wouldn't have to face the other women coming at a sensible hour. It is our sin, not theirs, that causes the ostracism.

The sin is one of desperation. We want to know that we are going to heaven. We are afraid of God's Judgment and the hell it could send us to. We are aware of our own unworthiness. We know we haven't done enough. The purest saints among us understand this better than the rest of us. Who but Saint Bernadette could have possible doubted her place in heaven? Only Saint Bernadette, close enough to heaven to know how unworthy even she was.

How comforting it would be to have a checklist. Do these things, and then you are a good person. Do these things, and you will be saved. If you do these things, repent for them. If you do these things, you will have God's blessing. How comforting the law was, in truth. Here is the way. Everything else is up to you.

Do these things, and you can relax about whether or not you are a good person and where you will spend eternity.

The summary the lawyer gives, then, is actually an *expansion* of responsibility. Now you must think, all your life, at every turn, how best to love God and your neighbor.

For some reason, we don't seem to believe, deep down in our collective soul, that we can love absolutely everyone in the world. We keep making up reasons why some people don't count. We keep making up ways of being cruel to them that don't count as "not loving" "our neighbor".

If we're not allowed to be racist or sexist anymore, if women and minorities are also our neighbor, if even the hated demographics of Romans and Samaritans and Muslims is denied to us...then surely we can still judge the sinners? Surely we are not meant to love them, or at least not meant to respect their life choices.

We want there to be exceptions to the two rules that sum up the law. Perhaps that is the real reason why the original version of the law is so long. Trying to sneak in provisions that allow us to stone men who lie with other men as they would lie with a woman (translation may mean prostitute) (Leviticus 20:13), or men who sleep with their mothers-in-law (20:14); or those who commit bestiality (20:15-16). But not, incidentally, people who cheat with/sexually assault their own slaves (19:20).

Now I have, at last, circled back to our woman. She has violated the precepts of the law. In my interpretation at the beginning of the chapter, I imagined her moving from the more socially acceptable ways of "ending" a marriage to the more frowned upon "divorce". Slowly, I imagine her moving out of the sympathies of her community as it all begins to look frightening and suspicious.

And then, finally, violating the explicit rules of the law by cohabitating with a man without marriage in the mix at all. Surely now, her shunning by the community was justified. She lived outside the law!

And yet she is our neighbor. That is what her neighbors forgot. That is what drove her to the well in the middle of the day, where she met Jesus.

Jesus, who was waiting for her at a time when only outcasts would go to the well. Waiting for the outcast among outcasts.

A Monologue To a Stranger

When I saw a figure sitting by the well, my steps slowed. All of a sudden, my feet felt heavy and my shoes oversized. It had been several months since I had endured a hostile stare as I drew water, but I tried to square my shoulders as I approached. If I showed that I could be hurt, it would only make matters worse.

As I drew close, I was surprised to see that the figure was a man. The timing make more sense. Some woman must have fallen sick and sent her son, who didn't know better than to wait until noon.

Then I recognized him as a Jew, and I confess that my heart leapt. It felt as if a weight had rolled off my sandals, and suddenly my feet could move with purpose once more. Because if this man was a Jew, then he was a stranger. And I sent a prayer that he would not leer at me, as men still did, for I am still pretty enough for my age. Let him be a kind, mostly disinterested stranger.

Let me have a small taste of human civility. Let me have a moment of kindness from someone with no expectation of seeing me naked. It would do wonders for my heart, I remember thinking.

I am shocked to realize, now, what a small measure of grace I would have settled for. What an insignificant blessing I would have cradled like salvation itself. When it was the real thing he came to offer me.

2 THE WOMAN OF SAMARIA

A Dialogue With a Jew

As I approached, I slowly remembered. Jews share nothing in common with Samaritans. Not food or drink or a kind word. The most I could hope for was a cold diffidence born of his ignorance. It would be more respectful, in some ways, than warm civility. Or so I told myself. Or so I sternly warned myself not to hope for actual human kindness.

He was watching me and I, him. Then I remembered myself. It had been so long since I had bothered to play the modest woman. So I averted my gaze and watched him from the corner of my eye, as the honored matrons of the town would have done with a strange Jew. I felt foolish. I had to sidle up to the well to avoid looking directly at him, swinging the jar at my side. And he probably wouldn't even be convinced by my playacting at respectability.

I nearly lost the rope in my surprise when he spoke.

"Give me a drink."

It was not the demand of a rich man, never dreaming he wouldn't be obeyed. My third husband was rich, and even when he wasn't anymore, he had rich friends. I know that voice of command and how they would have said those words.

Nor was it the plea of a man caught too long on hard times. I had fallen for that voice too many times to mistake it again.

6666

666666

There was neither command nor entreaty in his voice. He spoke as if offering me a choice.

A choice to be the kind of person who would give him water or not to be that person. To be the kind of person frightened of strangers or the kind to reach out to them. I wasn't frightened of strangers anymore, but I wasn't their servant either.

I looked up at him, surprised by his voice and all it seemed to carry. Heavy with weight, it was. So were his eyes. They looked right through me.

But that was just the thing. He didn't see a woman of Samaria, a natural enemy. Nor did he — nor could he — see a fallen woman. But he also didn't seem to see a woman, or not the kind he could dismiss out of hand. He looked at me, just another person sharing a small patch of earth with him. Waiting to see if I would share a drink of water as well.

When I was younger, I would have called the feeling I had then "naked." Exposed before a man with no way to hide. I know better now. I know that it was naked when I was most invisible. The real me. The woman with a mind and a heart. The person with thoughts and feelings. When I was naked I was just a body.

I had been a shadow, a ghost, for many years. Solidifying into a body when necessary, and then floating away again. Living my life from slightly outside my skin.

Suddenly I was present again. Solid. Soul and mind and body in one and fully visible to all. Not sliding away from the gaze of this strange Jew.

I blinked. He was a Jew. I, a Samaritan woman of ill repute. Jews and Samaritans share nothing in common. Even when they must share something as simple as a patch of dirt on a weary road, we were both supposed to pretend we weren't. He was not supposed to see me. Much less drag me back into my body and stare as the summer sun illuminated every wrinkle.

"How can you, a Jew, ask me, a Samaritan woman, for a drink?"

Have you ever tried to explain something to a child? Something simple, like why they have to go into a separate classroom than their older sister on their first day of kindergarten? Or why Daddy can't take her into the women's bathroom? Or why he can't play dress up with his older sisters? How long did it take you before you resorted to the equivalent of, "That's just the way it is"?

That moment is a taste of what waits for us on the day the Light of God shines upon us and we cannot hide any longer.

> And this is the judgment, that light is come into the world,
> and men loved the darkness rather than the light,
> for their deeds were evil. For everyone who practices
> wicked things hates the light and avoids it, so that his
> deeds may not be exposed.
> John 3:19-20

Children hold the reflected Light of God in this way. They haven't learned yet to hide in shadows. They see the world in a stark light that adults have learned not to see. We have built the shadows to hide the uncomfortable truths from ourselves. So that we can believe we are good people.

Children don't have that problem. Most of the outcasts don't either. That is part of what makes them the Children of God.

Let me try another story.

In C.S. Lewis's *Prince Caspian*, a character named Reepicheep tries to explain his code of honor to Aslan. To the five of you out there who have not read any of *The Chronicles of Narnia*, Aslan is Lewis's analog to Jesus. They are explicitly linked in the story, and Aslan serves the same function within the magical world of Narnia that Jesus does for Earth.

Reepicheep, a brave captain of an honorable band of fighting Mice held together through an exhaustive code of honor, tries to explain to Aslan why it's so important that his tail be restored to him after he loses it in battle. He is shamed to be without his tail in the presence of the Great Lion (Aslan). He stutters and stammers and makes himself look foolish and, all in all, seems roughly three years old in the process of trying to explain.

Trying to explain why Reepicheep would ever let any worldly, external thing give him permission to be who he really is. Why he would let something like a tail define his worth as a person. Why it really did matter

15

if he fit the image of a Brave Mouse that the world had created out of the random happenstance of history.

Why he would turn on a Brave Mouse, if one of his lieutenants had been the one to lose a tail in the battle.

I think it is that explanation that we will want to flee when the Light of God chases away the shadows in which we hide our sins. So that we can go back to pretending to already be good people. Or at least good enough people.

Someday, we will stand before God, who was there watching when the Israelites were taken captive and a poor remainder stayed behind and intermarried and kept the traditions of the faith going in the best way they could. He was there when the slaves were freed and returned to Judea. He was there in the first interactions of these people who used to be one people, and He was there in all the ones since. He watched the construction of all the walls they have built because they forgot they were one people.

God was there when they were one people. He knows exactly what built every invisible brick in the walls between them. Every sour look that fixed them in place.

That is what awaits us in judgment. Someday, we will have to explain to God why it is so important for us to be different races, ethnicities, genders, and nationalities. Why we have made the presence or absence of a tail the deciding factor in whether someone is good or worthless. Why it feels so important that we are Americans versus Europeans versus Africans versus Asians. Why we must define ourselves by something as foolish as a tail.

To a Being who remembers when we were all one people, we will have to explain this. To God, who knows that the world wouldn't end if we were one people again, despite what we seem to believe. To God, who knew and mourned each little stone we added to the walls dividing who we treated as worthy and who we cast out.

One day, we will stand in a Light more unforgiving than the blazing desert sun, and we will insist that it matters — Catholic and Lutheran, refusing to share salvation. American and Mexican, refusing to share prosperity. Heterosexual and homosexual, refusing to share marriage. Believers and atheists, refusing to share our image of the universe. Christian and Jewish and Muslim, refusing to share our commonly inherited

Lord God.

And we will look foolish.

Our answers will dry up on our tongues.

We will suddenly question things unspoken so long that we forgot that they were there. We will suddenly be forced to explain and justify choices first made generations ago that we have continued making without thought. We will stutter and stammer and try to explain and for once, God's face will not allow us to retreat into our shadows:

We've always done things this way.

It's not prejudice, it's just the way of the world.

I'm not saying they're ALL like that, but you've got to admit...

We've got to defend what's ours.

It's not like *I* set policy!

Our ancestors built this country.

Go back where you came from.

It's only fair!

It's just the way we do things, okay?

It has nothing to do with me.

That's just the way it is. It's not like we chose it. It just is.

These are the shadows that God's Light will chase away. We admit our overt sins in this life. Our own world doesn't allow us to hide when we violate its rules. We drag our evil men into the light when we find them. It's not all those ordinary sins that we will be humiliated to share on the Day of Judgment.

You want to practice for the day you stand before God? Find a child, and when they ask you about why we treat one person differently than another, why you live in a house and the man you just passed lives on the street, keep answering their "But why"s all the way down. Don't let yourself wrap up the ugly truth in a simple shadow of an answer, as you always do. Justify why there's a difference between black and white, gay and straight, man and woman, prisoner and free man, debtor and creditor, all the way down.

"But whoever lives by the truth comes into the light,
so that it may be seen plainly that what they have done
has been done in the sight of God."
John 3:21

That's what the Light will shine its harsh glare on. All the wicked deeds we pretend aren't all that wicked. All the terrible things in our world we stopped questioning when we grew out of being children.

Jesus doesn't see those reasons why it's okay to treat people like not-real people, and that is what He is about to explain to the Samaritan Woman.

She challenges Him directly: What are you doing? This isn't how we behave, Samaritan and Jew. The wall has been up between our people's for a long time. It must be there for a reason.

Jesus was there when the wall went up, stone by stone. He knows that not one stone of it is there for a *good* reason.

So He refuses to honor the prejudices on both sides. He refuses to be hampered by the divide between His Chosen People. Jesus refuses to be tied to the societal taboos we have established to keep ourselves apart from our brothers and sisters. He walked in our world, but He never helped to build our shadows.

And that's not all He will promise her.

Jesus doesn't stop at saying, "Look, you all need to stop being so silly about the whole Samaritan/Jew thing. It's really stupid, taking the long view of history. In a few decades you'll *both* be driven out by Rome anyway, so seriously, stop wasting time."

Jesus goes on to explain that He's out to bring down an even bigger wall.

The wall we built around the divine. The wall we built between ourselves and God.

All we ever had to do was ask, and God would rip the veil that separated the sanctuary from the outside world.

The Samaritan Woman is shocked that Jesus can hand wave the prejudices that have defined her life and her village and her people as she understood them all of her life. There are divides that even children don't need explained for them.

But if she knew who He was, she wouldn't be surprised that He could give a toss for all the worldly barriers we erected. Not when He will offer us a chance to tear down the silly barriers we built between ourselves and the true presence of God.

The barriers between Jews and Samaritans, the barriers between her and the rest of the village, the barriers between white and black, male and female, immigrant and citizen, prisoner and guard, are as nothing to Jesus. Because the barrier He crossed, just by being born, the barrier He would go on to shatter by His death and resurrection…All that makes our petty walls look like nothing.

We've been building the wall between the human and the divine so much taller. We've been afraid of direct contact with God for so long.

We all say we want guidance, but, if we're honest, we want a particular answer more than we want to know for sure that it's God's answer. We've been building walls around the sacred places and defining who's allowed through them and for how long for so many, many centuries. So many millennia.

A Samaritan Woman asks Jesus how He can pretend that the boundaries between Judea and Samaria don't matter. He responds that He came down to renegotiate the terms of contact between Heaven and Earth.

A Dialogue With A Crackpot

His eyes looked sad, but he smiled gently.

I expected him to puff out his chest, square his shoulders. Perhaps explain to me that since he is a Jew, an upright man, he has nothing to be ashamed of, unlike the trash of Samaria. For him to declare that everyone has a right to a drink and glare at me for getting in the way of his needs.

Or for him to start posturing about how he's not one of "those Jews" who care about such things. He's an Ally to the Samaritans. He wants to help the poor dears, is water such a lot to ask in return for that?

He did none of that. He just looked sad, and he smiled ruefully before he answered.

"If you knew the gift of God and who is saying to you, 'Give me a drink,' you would have asked him and he would have given you living water."

My first thought was how very, very long I had been thirsty.

How long it had been since I actually enjoyed a drink of the tepid water I hauled home every noontide. How long I had been thirsty for more than the cool water that could be teased from the well at dawn. For a simple nod of greeting as I walked up to the well.

But more now. I had been thirsting for his gaze. Not just anyone's glance, but his gaze. Right through me, fixing me to the present moment and solidly united in mind and soul and body.

For someone to look on me not with the speculative adoration of a potential lover nor the possessive leer of a man on the prowl nor the hateful spite of the faithful against one who has flouted the rules of society.

Just a person. Sharing a patch of dirt. Every bit as alive and vulnerable, as strong and worthy as you. Another soul moving in the world, seen as herself without shame.

I blinked. He didn't even have a bucket.

3 THE WOMAN DESCENDED FROM JACOB

A Dialogue With History

No bucket. Just a two-bit wise man about to make up some clever metaphor. Some city-slicker about to pull some oh-so-clever trick to show up the Samaritan bumpkin.

I disliked being played with under any circumstances. I had had enough of that in my life, and not only from my husbands. One of the things I liked most about my current man — for lack of a more official title — was his disdain of such games.

It had been a long time since I felt so angry at a man trying to show me up or string me along as if I were his entertainment for the evening. But this time felt like a betrayal. Like a promise his gaze made that his words had broken. That feeling of finally being seen, finally feeling present…just another tool in a petty confidence man's bag of tricks.

"Sir, you have nothing to draw with and the well is deep. Where can you get this 'living water'? Are you greater than our father Jacob, who gave us the well and drank from it himself, as did also his sons and livestock?"

Let him take the last bit about the livestock as he liked. If this Jewish man thought us all fools, thought me an ignorant woman who did not know even her own town's history, then his gaze had been paltry indeed.

I knew my history. I knew my Talmud. I knew everything I was allowed to know. I had been the curious young girl once, asking questions people would actually answer.

I hope I looked proud, but the truth is that I felt like weeping. I channeled it into my anger. I glared at him after my reply, so when he looked back at me, our eyes met.

His eyes met mine.

It had been so long since that happened. Did people always look so serious when they looked you straight in the eyes? Or was it just him?

And he was deadly serious. Accepting my anger and my scorn, but above all, accepting my presence. Accepting my right to be present on this shared patch of earth and feel all the anger I wanted. It felt wonderful to stand before him, defiant. Proud for the first time in so long. Demanding better treatment.

As I hadn't dared for so many years, worn down by my neighbors' disdain.

"Everyone who drinks this water will be thirsty again."

He meant the water in the well, but I think he meant my scorn and anger too. I think he meant my defiance and my pride.

"But whoever drinks the water I will give them will never thirst."

The Samaritan Woman's response is unquestionably a challenge.

In the passage above, I imagine her challenge as a defense of her own intelligence, civic-engagement, and sensibility. I imagine her trying to warn this crackpot stranger that she is not to be toyed with. She is no fool.

But I wonder if Jesus grinned when she stumbled — in her derision, her anger, or perhaps mere skepticism — upon precisely the right question. The very question, in fact, that He later has to feed directly to His apostles:

"But what about you?" He asked. "Who do you say I am?"
Mark 8:29

She may have been issuing a challenge, but when she says, "Who do you think you are?" she was asking precisely the question that Jesus has been waiting to answer.

Are you greater than our father Jacob?

Yes.

Perhaps it's even appropriate that the entirely wrong sentiment led her to the entirely right question. Isn't that one definition of grace? Stumbling upon the truth in the least likely place imaginable? Like the well at noon in a desert country.

Whatever prompts her to ask the question Jesus has to feed to his other disciples, He is able to jump straight to the answers with this woman. Instead of endless parables, He gives her one simple, blunt metaphor. He leaps straight to the heart of matters.

He explains that the well of the past, the water from a well precious to her limited tribe of people, the old way of connecting to God through lineage and ancestors and the surviving antiques of God's Chosen — will only make her thirsty all over again the next day.

The old ways of connecting to God aren't worthless, but they will satisfy her thirst for perhaps a day. A metaphor that has become a tragic symbol for everything else lacking in her life. Someone who pays so much each time she reaches for a drink understands well indeed how fleeting can be the comfort that more traditional religion gives.

Jesus proposes here and will eventually bring into existence a new kind of relationship with God — worship not on a mountain or in Jerusalem, water not from a historical well, not in any place she can be chased away from in shame, not in any place that could be trying to trick her.

Worship in her heart.

A supply of grace that renews itself within her. That will be her salvation and bring her someday to God Himself. A new kind of relationship with God that involves direct contact. No gatekeeping from the men who are so convinced they have accurately translated His divine will. Nothing that can be tainted by a community opinion which has poisoned her use of the well. One that shame cannot chase her away from. One that cannot be misunderstood by bickering theologians. A relationship with God that never leaves her thirsting.

He is promising the love of God, always with her. Something better than the well linking her to her ancestor Jacob indeed. Something better than an ancient promise: that promise finally fulfilled.

Who do you think you are?

Who do you say that I am?

Are you better than our ancestor Jacob and his promises of God's favor?

Yes, I am the fulfillment of the promise that he made.

A Dialogue With Hope

"Indeed, the water that I will give them will become a spring in them welling up to eternal life."

It was a metaphor, of course. How could it not be? The well is deep and old. This water would be new.

In that moment, I was certain he knew my thoughts. I couldn't guess how it was possible, but I believed it to be true. Was this man sent from God Himself? To free me from the shame of the well? A miracle for a small but everyday pain?

Or perhaps for even more. To give me a drink of human kindness that could sustain me forever. Dared I hope for that? A way of finding that kindness again, that love I had been craving so long. Craving so much I sought it in one man's bed after another.

Real love. Not the grasping, fading, dying kind I had known for so many years. And not only from my husbands. Not just the love of the community that had slowly been taken from me. Just love. Just-because love.

The words sprang from me as freely, as surprising, as the underground spring he had described.

"Sir, give me this water so that I won't get thirsty and have to keep coming here to draw water."

So I would never have to face hate and rejection again.

He looked me steadily in the eye, his jaw set, and I felt as if I could not move an eyelash.

"Go call your husband and come back."

I blinked.

He was no prophet. Not even a very good confidence man if he couldn't spot the town whore when she stood before him in the burning sunlight. He had never looked into my soul, if he thought I would bring a husband to meet him.

4 THE WOMAN WITHOUT A HUSBAND

A Dialogue With Honesty

"I do not have a husband."

I was going for proud and defiant again, but it doesn't matter how short I fell of the mark. The words were there, stark and plain. Naked. He would see nothing else now.

And there was no fire in my belly this time. Only the dull, empty ache of disappointment. An almost numb feeling. The only man to really look at me in years had only done so because he didn't know that I was the black widow of Samaria. I fell for some two-bit magician's trick, and he would never see me clearly enough to guess how much he had hurt me.

His kind eyes had seemed to see me and find me worthy. But only because he had no idea who I really was.

"You are right in saying, 'I do not have a husband.' For you have had five husbands, and the one you have now is not your husband."

I blinked.

This is the moment in this story when my heart always breaks.

Because every year of my life, I understand more what was done to this woman and what this moment means to her.

Because every year of my life, I understand a little more just how many people there are like her. People who have gone too long without human kindness. How many different ways we have invented to define people as unworthy of that kindness.

Jesus asks her to acknowledge her lifestyle, her sins, before He proceeds to grant her a direct line to grace. It must have been a heart-shattering moment for her.

And yet, which of us would respond with her calm bravery? How many of us would state, baldly, our defining worldly sin? Before a holy man? How many of us will answer so calmly, so without excuse, or so quickly on the Day of Judgment?

Especially since she must have thought, in that first moment, in her painful declaration, that the man who had looked at her and spoken to her as a person, as an intelligent and beloved child of God, was only doing so because He didn't know about her past.

This is when I wonder how long it had been since anyone had done that. Since anyone had treated her like a worthy person rather than a point of local gossip. Rather than a sinner to be shunned. Rather than an example of everything a young woman shouldn't be. I wonder just how long she had been alone. How many husbands ago did she stop feeling like anyone truly saw her?

She must have thought that His respect for her was about to evaporate in the face of her imperfect truth.

And no, she didn't spill everything at once. She did not have the courage to catalogue her sins and failings. She just admitted, sadly but proudly, "I do not have a husband." I am not the woman you think me.

Jesus's answer proved that He had unearthly knowledge, but the trick of omniscience is *so* secondary to what His answer really meant: that this prophet, this holy man, had known from the start that she was a woman with a "deplorable lifestyle", as the priest who accidentally inspired this book once called it.

He had known who she was, this woman more aware than most of her own unworthiness, from the very beginning. And still He had spoken to her. Still He had looked at her and asked for water from her hand. His love, His respect, His kindness…It hadn't been an illusion or a dream. It hadn't been a misunderstanding or the kind of treatment she could only get from a stranger.

This man knew her every sin and imperfection, every dark and twisty thing inside her, and loved her even so. Offered her God's love even so.

When she tells him, "I can see that you are a prophet," what she has actually realized is that the representative of God on earth is that kind of man: not the judging Pharisee or the self-righteous upright woman but the kind prophet by the well who spoke of God's love as a truth plain as day. Who took the task that was her daily shame and turned it into a metaphor for the strength and glory of God that He still saw within her.

The Samaritan woman was given a key to how to find the Light of God in other people. Those who saw her, those who treated her as a person — not as a charity case or a blight on a moral community — were God's true chosen people. She would know people of true faith by how close they came to this stranger — who could look at her, know everything she had ever done, and love and respect her just as if she had always been perfect.

Knowing her past was a cheap parlor trick in comparison to that gift.

A Dialogue With Understanding

He knew?

"What you have said is true."

I have tried many times to find the words for what I felt in that moment.

I sucked in a ragged breath, and if he had not caught the rope, my jar would have been lost in that silly well forever. I would not have cared. It was some time before I released my breath again. Some time, in which I tried desperately to make the last several seconds make sense. To comprehend that He, a holy man, a prophet of God, could know every sin I had made and still look at me as He had — with love and respect and belief that I could be worthy of living water. Worthy of the blessings of God.

"Sir, I can see that you are a prophet."

So why?

Why come to me? Not to a worthy woman of the town, full of honor and piety and holiness? I could have pointed you to any number of women reaching out for such as You day and night. If you know me, you must know them. I stopped daring to reach out for such as You oh, so long ago.

5 THE WOMAN SEEKING PEACE

A Question For a Prophet

Then came the thought: was everything we had thought about religion wrong? The rules, the binding laws, the judgments and the checklists for good behavior...were they all false?

Is God not like we thought He was? Does He not care about the location of our prayers? Are all the laws, all those excuses the village used to condemn me...nothing to Him?

I didn't quite have the nerve for that question yet. Instead I said, "Our ancestors worshipped on this mountain, but you Jews claim the place to worship is in Jerusalem."

He answered both of my questions.

"Woman, believe me, a time is coming when you will worship the Father neither on this mountain nor in Jerusalem. You Samaritans worship what you do not know; we worship what we do know, for salvation is from the Jews."

Despite myself, my heart sank a little. A holy man, blessed by God. A prophet. Spouting the same Jewish propaganda as the false ones. Apparently God was on their side, just as they claimed.

And then, as if he heard my thoughts again:

"Yet a time is coming and is now come when true worshippers will worship the Father in the Spirit and in truth, for they are the kind of

worshippers the Father seeks. God is spirit, and his worshippers must worship in the spirit and in truth."

The world around me looked the same. But I knew everything had changed.

A few weeks before I heard the homily that accidentally inspired this book, the professor of a playwriting class set us to answer a series of questions. They went on and on. Five ways you are similar to your parents. Five ways you are different than your parents. Five things you hate. Five things you love. Five people you would punch if you ever met them face to face. Five secrets you have kept. Five secrets you have not kept. Five people whose secrets you would always keep.

Five questions you would ask God if you met Him on the street.

It was not the first time I was asked some version of that question. It is, strangely enough, something of a go-to soul-searching prompt. We put it on the same level as "What would you grab first in the event of a fire?"

I don't remember any of the answers I wrote down for the professor or any of the answers I've given to different versions of that question over the years.

But I know that none of my answers have ever come close to the woman's question. None of them have been anywhere near as wise, anywhere near as important, or anywhere near as selfless as this woman's question.

The homily that accidentally inspired this book, the better homilies that have followed it, every reflection on the Woman at the Well that I have found since – all of them have interpreted the woman's question the same way. They imagine, over and over again, her desperate desire to change the subject away from her own "deplorable lifestyle". A way of dodging His difficult questions and the embarrassing knowledge He displays.

They imagine the divide over Jerusalem versus the Mountain of God to be a "safer" topic than her own, broken life.

We aren't seeing a desperate dodge. There are far safer topics out there than what this woman asks Jesus. We are seeing the one question she has chosen to ask the representative with a direct line to God.

If we could have one answer from God, what would it be?

I don't remember any specific answers I've given over the years. I think a true answer would be a petulant demand for why He took my father's life. Or I would ask after some trivia from the past. Or why did you build the system with so much pain built in? Or how to achieve some goal, probably spiritual, in this world. Or whether my loved ones are in heaven. Whether I will go to heaven one day. Even the visionary saints jumped straight to those last questions.

Without this story, it would not have occurred to me to ask what it would take to bring lasting peace to the Middle East. It would not have occurred to me to ask what I, personally, could and should do to shut down racism for good. I would have been too afraid to ask if I am right about His acceptance of homosexuality and my own bisexuality.

This woman was willing to risk learning that her people were wrong and their oppressors were right. She didn't ask after personal trivia or implore spiritual reassurances. She leapt straight to the central question that divided God's Chosen People. She wanted to know the truth behind the argument that kept the Jews and Samaritans divided.

Not how to get back in the good graces of the town. Not if she should stay with the man she lived with now. Not if God would forgive her for her sins. Not how her own life and conscience could be made to rest easy.

How to make her fractured people whole again.

She is, by instinct, a peacemaker and a seeker.

Of course, we could have guessed the latter from her personal history. She sought love in the arms of so many men who proved disappointments, but still she had hope in the truth of this man before her. She sought the Truth in the first place she had ever seen it offered.

My questions, in that situation, would be demanding Why. At their heart, that is what I want of God. My instinct is to ask Why. Not How, as this woman does. As the Virgin Mary did before her.

How can our broken people be put back together?

How can I heal hearts and minds?

How should I spend the days on earth you have given me?

How could I serve you better?

How can I be more than I am now?

Perhaps that's another reason that the outcasts are the blessed children of God. Perhaps this woman had the advantage over me, who has always had a strong community around her. Perhaps people like this woman grow used to asking: How can I win back your vanished love? How can I earn redemption in your eyes? How can I make you see me?

The woman at the well that day was curious and smart and brave and seeking peace. And everyone around her had stopped seeing it two husbands ago. Because her "lifestyle" was so "deplorable" that they stopped seeing the woman living it and saw only the facts of her life. Not the truth of her.

Her village had stopped demanding that she be better because they stopped believing that she could be. Somehow, by some miracle, the woman never came to believe it of herself.

Jesus saw all of that in her — the beauty of her soul. And if we can learn to look with His eyes, then we can see where He would lead us.

My question now will be: How can I be more like this woman, so that I may serve you better?

A Dialogue With the Messiah

"I know that the Messiah is coming. When he comes he will explain everything to us."

Because suddenly I wanted to know. Everything.

I had been afraid to ask for anything, about anything, for so long. I had been afraid of answers for so long, convinced that they couldn't be good or kind. All that fear was gone. I wanted to know everything.

He smiled at me again, kind but now a little amused. That I could not quite say what I really meant even now. I had been out of practice for so long.

"I, the one speaking to you, I am he."

He was the Messiah. Not the figure I had always imagined but this wise, holy, and good man. This man who saw me, through everything that made others turn away. This man with enough love for the cast offs like me. This man who came to me, the fallen and despised woman, condemned by the righteous who followed God's rules to the letter.

The Messiah was not like them, only even more full of holy fire ready to burn the wicked to the ground. The Messiah was the man who loved us all.

6 THE VOICE CRYING OUT
IN THE CENTER OF TOWN

A Monologue to Everyone

I felt a shout rising up within me. I could have leapt ten feet in the air. My feet almost took off without me, running for the town until they had placed me before every woman, man, and child to tell them who I had found. For so long, I had moved in shadows until I convinced myself it was better this way. I was wrong.

I had been so afraid of the light, but when I stood in it, I was free. And somehow beautiful, even with everything exposed. And for the first time, I saw the shadows that even the most upright and respectable had hidden themselves inside. And I wanted them to stand with me in the light.

For so long, I had felt as if I had been rendered dumb. As if even when I spoke, there was no one with ears to hear. That when I raised my voice, they heard only the whistling of the wind. But none of that was true. Always, always I had had my voice.

It must have looked to his companions as if I fled at their arrival, but my feet could keep still no longer. As I ran there was a spring in my step that flowed from the Spring in my heart.

Just like He promised.

By the time I hit the town square, the Spring in my heart was going off like a geyser trapped far, far too long beneath the dirt. Shooting out of the well without a bucket.

We had it all wrong, and everyone had to know. The love of God knew no bounds — not of geography, not of ancestry, not of codes of conduct invented centuries ago for a different world. His love was not earned by your adherence to a strict set of complicated behaviors and ceremonies. It was not a thing you could earn by any earthly act. Or lose by any earthly act.

It was a Spring of Living Water, unending and overflowing. All you had to do was drink.

"Come, see a man who told me everything I ever did. Could this be the Messiah?"

I phrased it as a question on purpose. It wasn't cowardice. I just knew my audience. Yesterday, I might have been offended that I had to pretend uncertainty for them to trust me. Today I did not care. Let the water flow from me to them in whatever way would help it reach their hearts. So that no one in our town would ever have cause to thirst again.

And as I ran from person to person with my pretended question, I spilled my water on the dry desert sands and the Spring in my heart only flowed forth more and more. Inexhaustible.

Come see a man who told me everything I ever did and loved me anyway. Come see a holy man who did not look down at me for my "fallen" state. Come see a prophet who knew my every fault and treated me only as a fellow child of God. Could this be the Messiah?

Could the Messiah be like this kind man? Not a figure of fire and judgment or punishment and war. Not a purging of all that step outside of the temple's narrow precepts, but a man who extends love to all, even knowing every fault.

Could this be the Messiah?
Could we possibly be that lucky?
Could we possibly be that blessed?
Could we possibly be that loved?

There's an image we have of Old Testament prophets. St. John the Baptist and Elijah and the rest. The Voice Crying Out in the Wilderness.

It describes John the Baptist directly in the gospels, but it's become my mental image of every male prophet. I don't think I'm alone in that, although perhaps most people don't distinguish between the male and female prophets. Or even think much about how there are and always have been female prophets.

But the women of the Bible and the female saints speaking truth to power through the last two thousands years look very different, by and large, from their male counterparts. We've had a few hermits like Julian of Norwich or Saint Faustina. But overwhelmingly the image of women of faith in this world is "A Voice crying Out in the Center of Town."

The saint I was named for, Catherine of Siena, doctor of the Church, can best be understood as the Voice Crying Out in the Papal Palace of Avignon. Mary, Mother of God, is the Voice Crying Out at the Foot of the Cross, in the Middle of the Angry Mob.

We need both kinds of prophet, of course, and the difference doesn't have to be gendered. But there's something interesting about the fact that, in our history so far, it seems to be.

There's value in traveling as part of your soul searching. There's value in retreating from the noise and bustle of the world to find God in the quiet. There's value in the people who remain in those calm, deep waters of faith to act as touchstones for the rest of us in our busy, bustling world.

There is also value in the people called to turn the Spring of Living Water in their souls into the Public Fountain in the Center of Town. Like this woman.

Most prophets get into trouble when they stand on the courthouse steps rather than the rock piles in the desert. Jonah was roundly mocked in Nineveh. It's when he started mentioning local politics that John the Baptist got his head put on the chopping block. Jesus's procession into the Jerusalem was the moment the Chief Priests decided that they definitely needed to kill Him.

It requires a kind of tact that the Voices Crying Out in the Wilderness usually lack to speak truth to power in the middle of an undecided crowd. Even Jesus came across the problem of a prophet being accepted everywhere but his hometown.

I think that's why the Samaritan woman phrases it as a question even when she knows better. The voices crying out in the center of town give testimony. They witness. They don't proselytize.

What's the difference? Giving witness is telling what you have seen. What you have known in your life. It's displaying for all the heart you have opened to God. It's not hiding your personal, deeply felt reasons for your faith. It's allowing the harsh light of communal judgment to shine on you.

Proselytizing is telling others what they should be doing. Trying to shine that bright light on others as well as yourself, often forgetting how blinding it felt at the first. Sharing the answers you believe you have found rather than the questions that led you there.

Witnessing allows for what happens next in the Samaritan village. Proselytizing, from a woman like her, wouldn't have worked. They would have dismissed her out of hand, and they would have missed their chance.

A few wouldn't have laughed her off, perhaps, but how many of us can honestly claim to be in that minority? Who among us truly doesn't care about the messenger so much as the message? When was the last time we took the time to really listen to those whom we judge and despise? Or simply look down upon?

Witnessing, on the other hand, invites you to hear someone else's story. No pressure, no judgment, no immediate statement that you are wrong and she is right. Just: "This is what happened to me. Come and see for yourself. Come, and ask the questions with me."

It invites people to experience and tell their own stories of faith. It invites people into the special club. Come and see, witness for yourself. I stand before you as witness to my own salvation. Not bearing aloft the rules and the one true way to faith that all should follow. Just the way that it happened for me. Just the thing worth seeking, perhaps, in your own way.

Her question invites the townsfolk to look at her and witness the change. To look on the evidence before them of her transformation. To witness the Light of God within her.

Proselytizing tries to tell you what is and what isn't God's will. Like John the Baptist to Herod. It was brave, it was honest, it was in service of God. It did not change Herod's mind.

It was an inspiration to those who already believed, certainly. It was an example of strength of conviction and a promise of God's strength in times of trouble, but it didn't change the mind of anyone. Voices Crying Out in the Wilderness bring hope and inspiration to those who already believe.

The Voices Crying Out in the Center of Town have a different call. Their witness invites you to see the answers for yourself and choose them for yourself. The Samaritan woman didn't come barreling into the midst of those who hate her and declare them all wrong and misguided. She merely came to them, brimming with light and love, and said, "I found everything I didn't know I was looking for at the edge of town. Come and see."

She invites them to open their minds and their hearts to God. She shows them how her heart was first opened and then filled. Then she invites them to come along.

So often these days everyone seems so certain. It's easy to dismiss their convictions. Everyone is so certain of so many contradictory things. They can't all be right. How can we trust anyone's answers?

We have forgotten that God is in the question.

We don't like absolutes in the modern world, but come to us with a question, and we take it up.

The woman at the well went into the center of town and invited people who had shunned her into the conversation as equals. And they came to Jesus and figured it out together.

We talk with such certainty of so many weighty things in religion these days. We are so certain of the answers. We declare the judgment of God with full confidence.

God is for America. God is with us in times of war. God hates fags.

If we followed a childish game of "Why?" down to the roots, would we find that these truths came from the Spring of Living Water in our hearts? Would we find the inspiration of the Holy Spirit at the roots of these teachings?

If we believe so, why are we afraid of the conversation?

Do we have the courage to truly ask? If we should worship in Jerusalem, as our enemies do, rather than the Mountaintop, where our ancestors have?

Why and then again why and then again why and still again why? With the innocent and the children and the outcasts pushing us still further down to the roots of the reason. Why? Why? Why?

Could this be the Messiah? Could the Jesus who died for us want these people to burn in hell? Could the God who created us have made a mistake? Could we find love without condition for people who break the laws of God? What does that look like? Is it "love" without political action? Without access to marriage? Without protections from being fired? Is it love that sends teenagers onto the streets to fend for themselves? Is it love that sends teenagers to reeducation programs?

If love is not denied to criminals, then why is the vote?

If God loves men and women equally, why can only men be priests?

If we are called to spread the good news to all people across the world, then why aren't they welcome in our home country?

If the poor are the blessed of God, why do we treat prosperity as a sign of God's favor? If the poor are the blessed of God, why don't we trust them to buy their groceries without restrictions? Why are we upset at them spending "our tax dollars"?

Is the Messiah really a figure of judgment? Of tribalism? Of nationality? Does God really take sides?

In the "Battle Hymn of the Republic," the second verse has a line that contradicts the overall message of the song. So certain the song is that God is on the side of the Union Army, for most of the song. In the third verse, "As He died to make men holy, let us die to make men free!" forever declares, on behalf of God, for the Union Army. And of the two, I'd guess that He was.

But in the second verse, there is a counterpoint:

> I have seen Him in the watchfires
> Of a hundred circle camps
> They have builded Him an altar in
> The evening dews and damps.

What a thing that is: to know that your God is also your enemy's God. That they are praying just as you are, and may be receiving the same answers. Or at least be as convinced as you are that the answers they have are from God. That He may watch over them the same as He watches over you. That He is in their watchfires just as much as in yours. That they have built Him an altar in their camp and in their hearts, just as you have done.

That they too are His children.

It is the woman's questions that bring the townspeople out to see the truth for themselves. They believe because they have seen for themselves. All she did was bring them to see that truth.

That sounds like a simple thing, perhaps, but in this world of ours, I can't think of anything that seems more impossible than convincing those who are certain of the truth to come and listen to something that could tell them that they are wrong after all. I can't think of anything harder than convincing those who believe the answer was written down millennia ago, in whatever holy book they follow, to ask the questions all over again:

Could this be the Messiah? This figure of peace? Who eats with tax collectors and sinners? Who chooses as His ambassador the black widow of Samaria? Could this be the Messiah? Who sees our sins and loves us anyway?

Could we possibly be that lucky? Could we possibly be that blessed? Could we possibly be that loved?

It's a beautiful message that comes with a fearful cost.

The woman at the well was not afraid to change her life. To change her religion. To change her outlook on the world. To change her self and her place in the world.

We are. But we needn't be.

I promise there will be pain, when the questions are finally answered. I promise there will be terror in the asking, when you finally ask as children do. I promise it will be hard and there will be a cost.

It's why it takes a great thirst for most of us to reach out for the Spring of Living Water.

I can offer no other promise, no true instructions. Only my own witness: There is a man on the edge of town who knows everything I have ever done, and loves me anyway. Who has seen into my heart and knew before even I did that it loves men and women the same. He has named me bisexual and loved me just the same. Respected me just the same.

He has seen me bully good people and corrected me. And He loved me all the while. He has seen me make my mistakes and treated me as His beloved child throughout. To the point where I thought my work on myself was done, until He gently showed me otherwise.

There is beauty in the words He says, even when they are hard. There is promise in the world as He sees it. There is water that can quench your thirst. There is water that can heal our world.

Each answer He gives is really another question, and the work is never done. His words are hard, and they demand things that cost, often far more than I want to give. But His love is there.

I have felt it. I have known it. It has changed me, and sustained me, and comforted me, and elated me, and demanded more than I thought I could give.

It has filled me with more love than I could have imagined.

A Dialogue With Everyone

A part of me, the part furthest from the Spring at the center of my soul, was surprised that they followed me. First one, then several. Perhaps after a time they were following each other rather than me. It didn't matter, so long as they came. It was better, that I was not the only Spring in town.

For two days, the Messiah was with our town. For two days, we asked our questions and He gave His answers.

For two days, I watched as the Spring of Living Water sprang up in one heart after another.

I watched as people with more to lose than I risked everything for their answers. I watched as life after life changed forever. I watched as the town I had known was destroyed and another was raised up in its place.

And there was pain, but there was also conversation after conversation like this:

"We no longer believe because of your word."

They had believed because of my word. Because of His words in me. Because of the power the Spring of Living Water gave to my words.

"For we have heard for ourselves. And we know that this is truly the savior of the world."

It was not some magic spell. It was not something born of my gratitude. It was something they too could see. The righteous and the ones like me. The rich and the poor. They saw and they spoke.

"We know that this is truly the savior of the world."

More than anything else, that was the gift. The relief of others believing too.

We are this lucky.

We are this blessed.

This is the man whom God has sent.
This is what we are called to be.
This is how we will save the world.

CONCLUSION

Let me propose an alternate parable.

<u>The Frog in the Ice</u>

Once upon a time and then repeated every ordinary winter, a tree frog in his natural habitat was content enough. Though he was growing increasingly concerned about the declining mosquito population in recent weeks.

All around the frog, the forest was going to sleep for the winter as the air and water grew colder. His fellows burrowed down into the soil and didn't return, but this little frog stayed in the world. He stayed in his tree.

Until, one day, the water around the frog froze solid.

But though the world seemed frightening, there was no cause to fear. The frog did not die. The frog waited in stasis until the world thawed and the ice melted and he lived his life again.

Besides the advantage of being scientifically true, this parable has much to recommend it over The Frog in the Pot.

Sometimes I think what really drives a fear of change is the idea that if we finally make it to perfect, we'll blow right past it. We'll keep going and blow our chance at the pinnacle of the curved line.

Some people, of course, believe we've already done that. That we had the perfect world and that we blew right past it.

What else drives modern dystopian literature but the fear that all this progress will reach the perfect world...then plow right ahead or dodge to the side and ruin it all again? That the perfect world in the future will only take up a small fraction of the future?

We want the world to be perfect and then freeze in place.

Or if not that, we want a list of rules that we can follow and know that we are safe. We want to know that we are going to heaven some day. We want Ten Commandments and 611 bylaws. We want to know that if we follow them, we will go to heaven. We want to believe that if everyone followed them, the world would become and then stay perfect.

We want the water around us to grow colder. To become more moral until everyone is abiding by the 613 or 621 laws (depending on how you combine the Ten Commandments with the Law of Moses).

We want to freeze, like the frog. We want our work to be over. We want the answers to have been decided for us. We want to rest in the knowledge that we are in the right. We are on the right path. We want the way of God and the path of righteousness to have been decided. We want to follow the Spiritual GPS instructions.

We don't want two rules that require us to constantly figure out what loving God and loving our neighbor really looks like in this brave new world.

We don't want the constant questions that have us jumping around the forest or the pot trying to figure out if the temperature is changing for the better or the worse. We don't want to have to risk getting the answer wrong and ending up boiling forever.

We don't want to have to keep asking if God is on the mountain or in Jerusalem. We want the questioning to be over. We don't want to continually ask, every day, with every person we meet, every cause we encounter, what is the way of love. We want a checklist of how we should treat our fellow humans.

We want a code of conduct.

Jesus came down to give us a rule of thumb. A guiding principle to decide for ourselves, in each new decade, in each new version of the world around us, what the path of love is.

Because the frog may not die in the ice the way it would in the boiling water, but it isn't truly alive either. It isn't needed for its ecosystem.

Neither are believers, in a world governed by set, unchanging rules.

Christ's followers are not needed in a world governed by set rules determining who is good and who is bad and what we need to do or not do to know ourselves as good people bound for heaven. We are needed in the lukewarm water, in the spring and the summer and the fall. Not to be lukewarm ourselves, forever uncertain and oscillating. That's just another form of laziness that Jesus rightfully condemned. But we are needed at the temperatures between boiling and freezing.

We are called to be in the world but not of the world. To be constantly questioning the world. To be constantly working within the world. We are called to be outside the world's set of rules governing behavior. Not as the self-righteous are but as our modern outcasts are.

We are meant to question the rules of the world at every turn. Even the precepts of our own religion, if the Spring in our hearts leads us there. So many of our saints did the same in their time. We forget that, somehow, when we honor the teachings that came from their questioning. Even their defiance of the Church of their time.

We are meant not for the frozen ice of a perfectly moral universe with easily understandable laws.

We are meant for the struggle and the questioning of how best to love. We are meant to continually challenge the ways and rules of the world in search of God's spirit.

We are meant for the living water that flows from a spring pure and light. Forever.

We are not meant to worry about the water's temperature. We are meant to follow where it leads. Wherever that may be.

ABOUT THE AUTHOR

Katy Mulvaney is a theatre teacher and writer in Houston, Texas. She is a cradle catholic, and proud member of the ACTS movement. She wrote *The Woman at the Well* while working on her MFA in Shakespeare and Performance from Mary Baldwin College. In addition to *The Woman at the Well*, she has also published a novella in blank verse on Delilah from the Book of Judges entitled *Lock by Lock*.

Made in the USA
Las Vegas, NV
20 May 2021